Please return this book on or before the last date stamped below.

1 4 FEB 2005

- 5 JAN 2015

- 5 DEC 2016

- 4 JAN 2017

PAGE PHILIP

FICTION GRE

D1470861

Hodder & St

A MEMBER OF THE HODDER HEADLINE GROUP

Acknowledgements
Cover: Doug Lewis
Illustrations: Philip Page

Orders: please contact Bookpoint Ltd, 78 Milton Park, Abingdon, Oxon OX14 4TD. Telephone: (44) 01235 827720, Fax: (44) 01235 400454. Lines are open from 9.00 – 6.00, Monday to Saturday, with a 24 hour message answering service. Email address: orders@bookpoint.co.uk

British Library Cataloguing in Publication Data
A catalogue record for this title is available from The British Library

ISBN 0 340 80012 7

First published 2001
Impression number   10 9 8 7 6 5 4 3 2 1
Year   2007 2006 2005 2004 2003 2002 2001

Typeset by SX Composing DTP, Rayleigh, Essex
Printed in Great Britain for Hodder & Stoughton Educational, a division of Hodder Headline Plc, 338 Euston Road, London NW1 3BH by Athenaeum Press, Gateshead, Tyne & Wear.

Aladdin

Contents

1

The Magician

Long, long ago there was a magician
who lived in Africa.
He read about a wonderful lamp
in his books of magic.
The person who found the lamp would be
rich – the richest person in the world.
The magician had to have it.

For many years he searched the world
for the lamp.

At last he found where it was hidden.
It was in a deep, dark cave in China.

The magician knew that he could not
take the lamp himself.
It had to be given to him.
If he just took it, the magic would be lost.

'There is a city a day away,'
said the magician.
'I'm sure I can fool somebody
there into helping me.'

Now in this city lived a poor widow
and her son.
The boy's name was Aladdin.
His mother worked hard
but Aladdin was lazy.
He did nothing. He just sat
in the market place all day long.

It was there that the magician saw him.
'He looks lazy and stupid,'
the magician said to himself.
'It will be easy to get him to help me.'

The magician went up to the boy.
'Is your name Aladdin?' he asked him.
'Yes,' said Aladdin.
'And was your father a tailor?'
Aladdin said he was.

The magician smiled.
'I knew your poor father many years ago,'
he said.
'I came to China to see him.
I am sad to learn my old friend is dead.'

Aladdin took the magician to his home.
'We are poor,' his mother said to the magician,
'but you are welcome to stay
and eat with us.'

'I would like to help you,' said the magician.
'After all, you are the family of my old friend.'

He told them he knew where
some treasure was buried.
He asked Aladdin to help him find it.
He told them they would all be rich.
He did not say anything about
the magic lamp.
Aladdin could not wait to go
in search of the treasure!

2

The Ring and the Lamp

Early the next day Aladdin
and the magician set off.
Soon they had left the city far behind.
They began to walk up into the mountains.

The day was hot and Aladdin was tired.
'Is it much further?' he asked.
'My feet hurt.'
'We are almost there,' said the magician
'Good,' said Aladdin. 'I'm hungry as well.'

At last they came to a valley.
Tall cliffs cast dark shadows on the ground.
'We are there,' said the magician.
'I don't see any treasure,' Aladdin said.
He was tired and fed up.

'Watch!' said the magician.
He closed his eyes
and said some magic words.
A large rock in front of them
rolled to one side.
Aladdin saw a square stone in the ground.
It had a large metal ring fixed in it.

'Lift up the stone,' the magician said.
Aladdin pulled the ring.
The stone came up easily.
Under the stone Aladdin saw some steps
going down into the ground.

The magician told Aladdin to go down
the steps.
'You can keep anything you find down there,'
he said.
'There is only one thing I want.
If you see an old oil lamp,
bring it up to me.'

Aladdin did not like the look of the
dark stone steps.
'I don't want to go,' he said.
The magician took a ring from his finger.
'Here,' he said. 'This ring is worth
a lot of money.
Take it as payment for going down there.'

Aladdin took the ring.
He went slowly down the steps.
The air became colder.
Cobwebs brushed his face.

The steps led down to a large cave.
At the end of the cave was a door.
Aladdin opened it slowly.
He saw another, smaller room.
But he could not see any treasure.

Inside this room he saw a stone table.
On the table was an old oil lamp.
He picked up the lamp.
Then he went back to the bottom of the steps.

The magician was waiting.
Aladdin thought he looked very excited.
'Did you find the lamp?'
shouted the magician.
'Yes,' said Aladdin. 'But where's the treasure?
Give me the lamp and I'll tell you.'

'No,' said Aladdin. 'Tell me first.'
The magician became very angry.
'Give me the lamp,' he screamed.
Aladdin shook his head.

'Then stay there and die,'
yelled the magician.
He said the magic words and the rock
rolled back over the hole.
Aladdin was trapped.

He shouted.
He screamed.
He burst into tears.
He put his hands together
and started to pray.

As he did so he rubbed the ring
the magician had given him.
There was a bright flash of light.
A strange man floated in the air
in front of him.

'Who are you?' Aladdin gasped.
'I am the Slave of the Ring,' the man said.
'Make a wish and I will grant it.'

'I wish I was out of here and back home,'
said Aladdin.
There was a flash of light
and a roll of thunder.
Aladdin found himself standing outside
his own front door.

'Where did you come from?'
asked his mother.
She was surprised to see him.
'And where's your father's old friend?'

Aladdin told his mother
what had happened.
'So there's no treasure,' she said.
'And we've got no food.'

'I've got this old oil lamp,' said Aladdin.
'We can sell it and buy a loaf of bread.'

His mother gave him a piece of cloth.
'Give it a good polish,' she said.
'You might get more for it if it looks clean.'

Aladdin began to rub the lamp
with the cloth.
Suddenly, the lamp began to shake
in his hand.
Green smoke began to curl up out of it.
The smoke got thicker and thicker.
Then slowly it turned into a tall, green genie!

Aladdin and his mother were terrified.

'I am the Genie of the Lamp,'
the genie said in a low voice.
'Your wish is my command.
Ask whatever you want
and I shall give it to you.'

3

The Princess

Aladdin could have wished for anything.
But he was happy to ask the genie
for just enough money to buy food
and clothes for him and his mother.
Aladdin knew what it was like to be poor.
But he was not greedy.

Two years passed.
Then one day the king's soldiers
came into the city streets.

They told everybody to lock themselves
inside their houses.
The king's daughter was coming.
Nobody was allowed to look at her!

Soon the streets were empty.
All the doors and windows were shut.
But Aladdin wanted to see what
the princess looked like.
He opened his door just wide enough
to look out.

He saw the princess as she passed.
She was the most beautiful woman
he had ever seen.
He fell in love with her.
He told his mother that he wanted
to marry her.
'Don't be stupid,' his mother said.
'She is a princess. She won't marry you!'

Aladdin rubbed the magic lamp.
The genie appeared.
'What do you want, my master?'
he asked Aladdin.
'I want to marry the princess,' Aladdin said.

The genie laughed.
'I can do most things,' he said to him,
'but I cannot make a woman love you!'

For days and days Aladdin did not eat.
He lay on his bed and would not go out.
He did not speak to anybody.

His mother asked him what the matter was.
'I love the princess,' said Aladdin.
'I don't want to live if I can't marry her.'

His mother rubbed the magic lamp.
She asked the genie to give her a golden box
full of jewels.
Then she went to the king's palace.

Every day for two weeks
she stood outside the palace.
At last the king noticed her.
He sent for her and asked her
what she wanted.

'My son wishes to marry the princess,'
said Aladdin's mother.
'So do many young men,' replied the king.
'They have brought presents of gold and
silver to give her.'

'My son sends her this present,' said
Aladdin's mother.
She opened the golden box.
The king was amazed at what he saw.

'Your son must be very rich,' he said.
'He is,' replied Aladdin's mother.
'Come back tomorrow with your son,' the
king told her.
'I will let him speak to the princess.'

Aladdin's mother rushed home.
She told her son what the king had said.
'But the king expects you to be a rich
man,' she added.
'I shall be', said Aladdin.
And he rubbed the lamp.

The next morning Aladdin went
to the palace.
But he did not look like a poor widow's son.
He was dressed as a prince.
He rode a beautiful white horse with a silver
saddle and bridle.
A hundred slaves followed behind him.
They were dressed in silks and gold.
Each slave carried a basket of jewels.
The genie of the lamp
had granted all his wishes.

The king liked what he saw.
He had never seen such riches.
He took Aladdin to see the princess.

The princess did not take any notice
of the gold and jewels.
She saw only a handsome young man
who smiled at her.
She fell in love with Aladdin as soon
as she saw him.

Aladdin took her hand in his.
He knelt before her.
'I have come to ask you to marry me,'
he said.
The princess blushed.
'I will marry you, if my father, the king,
agrees,' she replied.

The king was still looking
at the baskets of jewels.
'Yes, you can marry,' he said.
'But where will you live? The princess
is used to living in a palace, you know.'

'I will build a palace for her,' said Aladdin.
'That's another job for the genie of the
lamp,' he thought to himself.

4

New Lamps for Old

The genie of the lamp built a wonderful
palace for Aladdin and the princess.
People came to gaze in wonder at it.
Gold shone on its walls.
The furniture was bright with jewels.
The curtains were made of rich silk.
The air was sweet with perfume.

Aladdin and the princess were married.
They lived together happily for they were
very much in love.

Then the magician came back!
He had heard that Aladdin
had married a princess.
He had heard about the wonderful palace.
He knew that Aladdin must have used the
magic lamp.
Now he was angry and jealous.
He wanted the lamp.

He thought of a plan to get it.
The magician dressed up
as an old lamp seller.
He waited until he knew Aladdin was not
in the palace.
Then he pushed his cart full of lamps
to the gates of the palace.

'New lamps for old.' he called out.
Soon, a crowd gathered.
'Are you crazy?' people said to him.
'Are you really giving away brand new lamps
for old ones?'

'Yes', said the magician. 'I love old lamps.'
People rushed back to the homes to get
their old lamps.

A servant told the princess
what was going on.
'Your husband has an old lamp,' the
servant said.
'Why don't you get a new one for it?'
'Why not?' said the princess.
She did not know the lamp was a magic one.

The servant took the magic lamp
to the magician.
'Will you give me a new lamp for this
one?' she asked.
The magician snatched the lamp from her.
'Take any lamp you like,' he laughed.
'Take them all if you want!'

When Aladdin returned, the palace and the
princess had disappeared.
He stared at the empty ground in panic.
He had to find the princess. He loved her.
'Where is my old lamp?' he asked the servant.
'I gave it to an old lamp seller,' the
servant replied.
Aladdin knew it must be the magician.
Who else would have know about the
magic lamp?
The magician had taken his lamp,
as well as his wife and his palace.

Aladdin rubbed the ring on his finger.
The Slave of the Ring appeared.
'What is your wish, master?' he asked.
'Take me to my wife,' said Aladdin.

In the blink of an eye Aladdin was on the
top of a high mountain.
He saw his palace in the valley below.

When night came he went to the palace.
He climbed the wall to his wife's room.
When the princess saw him,
she burst into tears.
'I thought I would never see you again,'
she sobbed.

Aladdin told her about the lamp.
'So that is why the magician keeps it with
him all the time,' the princess said.
'Has he harmed you?' Aladdin asked.
'He says he will kill me if I don't marry
him,' said the princess.

'I will be back tomorrow evening,'
said Aladdin.
'I know how we can get rid of him.'

The next day Aladdin ordered the Slave of
the Ring to give him some poison.
That evening he took it to the princess.
'Put this in the magician's wine
when you eat with him,' he told her.

'Be nice to him, make him think you like him.'
'That will be hard,' said the princess,
'but I shall try.'

The next day the princess kept smiling
at the magician.
He thought she had changed her mind
about marrying him.
Later, she put the poison in his cup
and also in hers.

'Let us drink to our happiness,'
said the magician.
Then he took the princess's cup.
The princess put his cup to her lips.
but she did not drink any of the wine.
The magician drank all of his wine.
A few minutes later he was dead!

When Aladdin came back he took the lamp from the dead magician.
He rubbed it and the genie appeared.

'Why did you take away my wife and my palace?' Aladdin asked.
'I serve whoever has the lamp,'
said the genie.
'Then serve me now,' said Aladdin.
'Take us and the palace back to China!'

There was a crack of thunder.
A great wind roared.
The palace shook.
A moment later they were back home.

Aladdin never lost the lamp again.
He and the princess lived happily for the rest of their lives.

And what became of the magic lamp?
Nobody knows!